REMEMBER ME
The Story of My Life

SUSAN CAPURSO

Red Penguin Books

ISBN 978-1-949864-35-9

Copyright © 2019 by Susan Capurso

All rights reserved.

No part of this book may be reproduced in any form or by any electronic or mechanical means, including information storage and retrieval systems, without written permission from the author, except for the use of brief quotations in a book review.

REMEMBER ME
The Story of My Life

Love Forever, _____

To my boys, Jimmy and Jesse, who since the beginning of time, have never questioned me on any endeavor I chose to pursue and had my back no matter what the outcome.

To my late Husband, who since the beginning of our time, not only modeled the behavior above, but from Heaven, started me on the sacred Journey I am on today.

To my Aunt Patty, who's been with me since the day I was born and loves me more every day.

To my very Good Friend, my Cheerleader, Mentor, Confidant and Teacher. A humble example who's given me the strength to wake up, move forward and work hard to achieve anything in this lifetime.

Welcome!

Thank you for being mindful and leaving a piece of yourself for so many generations to come. Dedicate your work of art to one single person, to your family, a friend or for every generation to come in the future.

When you scroll through the pages, try to write your passages in the order they are in. Your process in remembering will lead you from the child you once were, to the person you've become today. Your words will carry on. Take your time with this project. Do the work so you can complete this properly. Put your pen down, process the information and try to remember the little details. A hundred years from now or six generations after you, this will be picked up by a person longing to know history. What were things like back then? How did people think and feel? What kinds of clothes did they wear? What did they do for work, how did they spend their free time? What inventions did they have that are outdated now? So many questions fill the minds of so many people. Yes, we can ask Mr. Google many things. It's not quite the same as picking up a written treasure that captures wishes, dreams and desires.

You have the opportunity to do this here. I've tried to mix it up and give you a thorough block of prompts for you to utilize. I'm sure there are pieces missing, however, I've given you ample subjects to explore and journey into your own past.

Understanding the meaning of our lives is a question many of us never find the answer to. Appreciation is key. Through self-awareness, mindfulness, reflecting and being grateful for each and every day, we are able to realize how life comes full circle. Don't waste another minute, you may think you have time, until you don't. Button things up, leave things in order and leave your mark on the world.

We all have a story inside of us. Review your life, relive good memories, empower and stimulate your mind. Validating your feelings and memories is vital. Sharing stories is powerful for both you and the reader alike. We've all had hardships, good times, blessings and decades of detailed memories that are worth sharing. The wisdom and perspective you have to offer all of us, priceless! Reliving old memories and passing down your experiences is a thumbprint you can leave on the world. You will have completed a treasure to last many generations to come. It is a gentle reminder of having lived a loving and full life. Enjoy your ride!

(Your) DEDICATION

DEAR, _____

Remember me when I was young, remember me when I am old. So many stories in my life yet most were never really told.

I hope in some small way, you are just like me, I wouldn't be surprised as we're from the same family tree!

As I leave a thumbprint of my life, I'm hoping you will see, every story and thought we leave behind is part of family history! Enjoy!

LOVE, _____

Today's Date:

_____

Full Name:

_____

Where I was born: _____

My Birthday! _____

NOTES:

_____

_____

_____

_____

_____

CHAPTER 1
A SUMMARY
THROUGH THE YEARS

If you can't fill in the blocks that are older than you are now, skip them and move on to the next section.

My earliest memory before I was five, how great it was just to be alive. We are so innocent, so vulnerable and true, I want to share these glimpses with you.

I was born in _____ and lived my first five years in _____.

_____
_____
_____
_____
_____
_____
_____
_____
_____
_____
_____

Soon nearing ten, I'd spend my days, mostly at my school (name)_____. I couldn't wait until I got home, all I wanted to do was play.

(I lived in _____, A small town in _____).

My favorite things to do when I played outside were:

_____
_____
_____
_____
_____
_____
_____
_____
_____
_____
_____
_____
_____
_____
_____
_____
_____
_____
_____
_____
_____
_____
_____

Here comes fifteen, I really knew it all, no longer little, I was growing tall. If you asked me what I did, or how I spent my days, the memories that come to mind are really clear as day. (I lived in _____, a small town in _____).

Soon I'm turning twenty, I'm really grown up now, how I even got here, I don't remember how! I do know who my friends were and what we used to do, I'd love to go back in time to share a memory or two.

I hung around with _____ a lot!

(I lived in _____, a small town in _____).

We loved to:

_____
_____
_____
_____
_____
_____
_____
_____
_____
_____
_____
_____
_____
_____
_____
_____
_____
_____
_____
_____
_____
_____

I'm almost twenty-five, and I felt really alive! My days were filled with wonder, my nights were filled with fun, if you only could have known me, my life had just begun! (I now live in _____, a town in _____)

Late twenties into thirties, life was different, no longer a kid. Let me tell you a story, some of the things I did!

(Living in _____, a small town in _____).

Later in my thirties, Forties sneaking up too soon, I always looked into the sun then suddenly see the moon. Sometimes were tough but others good, I tried to find my way, I'd wake up every morning and look forward to a brand-new day.

(Living in _____, a small town in _____).

S oon forties turning fifty, how did these numbers rise? I guess I'm now a giant grown up, you can see it in my eyes. If you don't know me, if you can't see how, I'll tell you the story of how I got here now.

(Living in _____, a small town in _____).

_____

L ate fifties turning sixties, uphill all the way, the ups and downs I've travelled, I have still have much to say. If your still here on my journey, and you have an ear to lend, I'll tell you a little story, I'm still far from my very end.

(Living in _____, a small town in _____).

L ate sixties turning seventy, my life is flying by, I'm always asking the question, "Why, oh why, oh why?" Just remember –

(Living in _____, a small town in _____).

My train is traveling faster, the eighties will soon be here, let me tell you honestly, I do have several fears. They may not be the fears you think, the ones that worry you. My fears in life are smaller now, I will share them all with you.

(Living in _____, a small town in _____).

I made it through the eighties with ninety on the rise, the heat is on I know it, not to my surprise. I live life to the fullest, was this all a test? I've tried to live it mindfully and do my very best. You should know this about me now:

(I live in _____, a small town in _____).

_____
_____
_____
_____
_____
_____
_____
_____
_____
_____
_____
_____
_____
_____
_____
_____
_____
_____
_____
_____
_____
_____
_____

I made it to a hundred, three digits I must say, I still have fun, a different kind and still really love to play. If you've made it here and you see my words, focus and stay clear... as any human who's turned a hundred years old, still has advice for you to hear!

(I am now living in _____, a small town in _____).

My nationality is _____ and my ancestors came from _____ and _____. My last name is a good one: _____, I think it means _____, and is originally from _____ .

I'll leave a little history; what I know I'll share. A little bit of background, is what I'll tell you here.:

_____

_____

_____

_____

_____

_____

_____

_____

_____

_____

_____

_____

_____

_____

_____

_____

_____

_____

_____

_____

_____

_____

_____

_____

_____

If I could summarize my life in only five lines, I'd have to tell you this, a summary in my mind.

1. _____

2. _____

3. _____

4. _____

5. _____

I was born in the year _____. If I could tell you about five life changing events for me, I'd have to say that these were key.

1. _____

_____

_____

_____

2. _____

_____

_____

_____

3. _____

_____

_____

_____

4. _____

_____

_____

5. _____

_____

_____

_____

My Grandparents were special; you'd love them for sure. I'll share a few memories; I wish I knew so much more.

My Mom's Side:

_____
_____
_____
_____
_____
_____
_____
_____
_____
_____

My Dad's Side:

_____
_____
_____
_____
_____
_____
_____
_____
_____
_____

My Mom and Dad were sometimes fun but certainly serious too, I'll never forget a particular time, something you never knew.

It drove my parents crazy when ...

On most days, my Mom could be funny and so very sweet, let me tell you a few things about her life and what she meant to me.

Sometimes serious, I loved my Dad, he really stood out in time. A few occasions I want to share, there's one that stands out in my mind.

Brothers and Sisters, good memories and bad, most times were happy, sometimes we were sad. I remember a story that stands out in my mind, I have to say this is one of a kind.

Spring, Summer, Winter and Fall, we can like one season, we might love them all. When I think of the past and the seasons gone by, I do have a favorite and I will tell you why.

Some people like the mornings, the smell of eggs and toast, others like the lunch bell, escape on every coast. So many like the evenings, a calming close to the day, me I had my favorite and wouldn't want it any way. My favorite time of the day is the _____. I like it best for so many reasons:

Most of us work or even go to school, on a day home alone, it was really cool. What did I love? What did I do? How would I spend my day? As memory has it, a free day alone, what more can I possibly say! I can remember ...

When I was young and home at night and my family was all together, I remember most the things we did and feeling light as a feather.

I remember my bedroom, a hard thing to do, was it old and real messy or shiny and new. Did I have lots of things or hardly any, did I have any posters or not very many? When I think of my room where I slept and had dreams, I remember the colors, the sheetrock and beams. I remember the things I'd do there the most, I'll tell you the good things and leave out the ghosts!

We all had our toys, our favorite obsessions, life wouldn't be life if we didn't have our possessions. Dolls, cars, barbies, GI Joes, a few of my favorites, now you will know.

Playing games is a pastime we know; competition is healthy and free. Monopoly, Cards or Parchisi it could be, I'll narrow it down and tell my top three.

1. _____

2. _____

3. _____

Home is where the heart is, a safe place for you to be. My memories of being there, I'd like you all to see. The rooms in the house, the yard in the back, a part of who I am. I'll share with you, it seems so clear, such memories that I hold so dear.

Some of us had animals, some have to go without, I remember all the animals I had, a story I'll tell you about.

We all have memories of our days in school, some stand out in the crowd. Field trips, friends and homework too, some flashbacks are so loud.

Was I clever, cute or mean? Our personalities so diverse. Was I kind, playful and free or filled with attitude, how can that be? I wasn't a trouble maker, I cannot lie, I will be honest and dig deep inside.

Broken bones, injuries, I know I had a few scraped knees. When I was sick I had chicken soup and my Mom made tea and toast, but of all my sickness and the boo boo's I had, I'll tell you what I remember most:

I could smell the rain on a rainy day, I can smell clean sheets and the month of May. I can smell the flowers in a vase, I can smell fog in the evening haze. But most of all, the smells I recall, the sauce and baking, anything Mom was making! Everything she cooked was enough to make us stop, I had a few favorites that made it too the top. My favorite smells, food and kitchen memories:

What about church or Temple? Did I believe? I'll tell you a little, I'll help you to see what I see - My thoughts on religion, spirituality and my personal beliefs:

Cookies for Santa, New Years ball at midnight, so many traditions like flying our kites. We all have good memories of the things we used to do, then there were others, we wish no one ever knew. Of course, there was love, the warm and the hugs, but then the stupid stuff, we pushed under the rug. I remember the good, the shiny and new, but what you don't know is this ... and I'm here to tell you:

Cartoons on Saturdays, family movies at night, after school specials, some dark and some light. My favorites were great, I always loved the best, "The Sound of Music," so much better then the rest. There was "Willie Wonka," the "Three Stooges" too. I had so many favorites, let me share with you:

Some people love to paint or draw all day long, some people love to sing and belt out a song. Was I creative, what did I love to do? A few things to tell you, I bet you never knew.

_____
_____
_____
_____
_____
_____
_____
_____
_____
_____
_____
_____
_____
_____
_____
_____
_____
_____
_____
_____
_____
_____
_____
_____
_____
_____

Somehow life was different, we stayed outside all day, we didn't come in until dinner, all we wanted was to play. Our parents didn't worry or hover over us, I think we had more freedom, no seatbelts on the bus. We played kickball, we played with rocks and dirt, we played outside in nature, we hardly ever got hurt. Things were pretty easy, if you only knew, these are some of the things, I really loved to do.

Food is good, food is love, food was sent from up above. We have our favorites, more than a few, and if we didn't cook, we had McDonalds too. Spaghetti and meatballs, macaroni and cheese, all the good stuff, I just couldn't get enough. Yummy foods are a must, be sure you have a list, comfort foods are key in life, never to be missed. *Foods I loved, Love and Always Will Love!*

Never really scared, I think I'm pretty tough. But sometimes things in life, can get a little rough. I try to keep positive, not think about worries or fears, sometimes it's hard, I've had a few throughout my years.

Events in our lives change the road ahead, people in our lives, some here and some dead. Life brings us change, nothing stays the same, although our timeline moves forward, our being still remains. We can move with the tides, move forward in life, or crawl in a hole and give in. Continue your journey and pick yourself up, teach yourself how to begin. The biggest changes I've endured in life:

___
___
___
___
___
___
___
___
___
___
___
___
___
___
___
___
___
___
___
___
___
___
___

I'm more like my Mom, no ... more like my Dad, maybe some of both. My eyes are all his, my Mom gave me strength, I guess it's a combo, a mixture, I think. I'll tell you a story, one you'd like to hear, I'll tell you who I've followed down the road all of these years. Our parents bring us to the world, their DNA in tow, learning more about my genes may help more than you know.

Some kids went to Disney, some just to visit an Aunt, some lay on a beach for a week, while others went off to camp. Me, our family was different, our favorite vacation a breeze, we dressed like monkeys and found a forest and swung from all the trees! Kidding! The places we'd go:

We all had a hero, everyone does, mine was not Barbie and definitely not Buzz. I looked up to my hero, so brave and so strong, I bet you'd never guess, if you did, you'd be wrong. There are many heroes we seek from close or afar, fantasy or family, could be a Movie Star. Some will stand the test of time, I wanted to share a few of mine.

I couldn't wait for holidays; we'd get to play and rest. Being with my family and friends, was the very best. I'd like to tell you now, the one I looked forward to most, I still to this day enjoy that day, almost better than Moms French toast!

Parenting is hard, I know first hand it's true, some parents are nice and sweet, some others a bit cuckoo. When I think how I did, I'll certainly tell the truth, some days were simply heaven on earth and others like a painful wisdom tooth!

When I was little, who ever knew, the most fun I had and thing I loved to do. It made me smile and fill up with joy, I loved it more than any of my toys!

There were things in life that made me mad, things in life that made me sad. I'd think of these memories, time and again, I really don't like to remember them.

I loved my cousins, we had lots of fun, our adventures were great even before they had begun. Of the greatest memories I keep in my mind, the laughing and screaming, the happiest times:

I'm easy to get along with, I rarely get mad, there's a time I remember that was really so sad. I begged and I pleaded, my parents said no, this hurt me and scarred me, more then they know.

Music is treasure, a gift of all time. My favorites, I love them and they are all mine. If I were in a room and could listen all night, what music's in my heart, what music's in my sight?

Life does happen, some things we can't change, we don't mean for them to happen, they just re-arrange. It was an accident, I really do swear, I didn't mean to do it, I really did care. It could have been worse, I'm grateful for that, I'm happy today, I never look back.

I love presents, gifts and shiny things. I love games, toys, jewelry and rings. When I think way back, it wasn't that new ball, the present I loved most made me happiest of all!

Money can be bad, but mostly it is good, money growing up, I knew just where we stood. Everything we needed, we always seem to have, if I was wrong, we never felt any lack. I'm so thankful for:

In elementary, we were taught to read, our knowledge in words, the way to succeed. My parents, my teachers, all the crazy looks, I'll tell you how I really felt reading all those thousands of books! And my favorites were ...

The inventions were enormous, all through the years, some of them were stupid, the good ones brought you to tears. Computers and phones, Bluetooth and TV, some of the best were great and really important to me.

You wouldn't believe my very first job, I'm not sure if I liked it, but didn't act like a snob. I know that it's important to love what you do, so through my experience, I'm hoping to give a tip or two.

I learned to be loving, I was taught to be kind, I tried to be humble, I walked a straight line. If I could give credit, who would it be, they taught me so many loving qualities. Thank you _____, I'll always be grateful. You taught me:

Baseball, Hockey, Football or Dance. Cheerleading, Cooking or Kickball by chance. Was it golf or Art or Chess Club for me? What sport did I love, which one could it be?

Birthdays are cake, balloons and a song, I've now had so many, I could have counted wrong. If I had to think back to the best one of all, this would be the one, I'd have to recall.

The snow was five feet, when I went out to play, I didn't feel cold at all. I felt really warm and took off my coat, I could have stayed out all day long. Zero degrees didn't matter, life was so fun to me. The things I remember, I want you to see. I'd love to share my memories.

O ur clothes can define us, tell people who we are, I'd like to think I dressed well and that I raised the bar. I'm really not so sure, I didn't choose my clothes, was I cool, was I chic I'll really never know. What I do remember is this:

Did I lie, did I cheat, did I steal from a store? These things I don't want to remember, the things I want to ignore. One does stand out, so vivid and true, for the sake of generational education, I'll share it with you:

If I could give my younger self a tiny piece of advice, I'd tell them to listen, I will be very nice. Share this with family, your children, your friends. An older person's wisdom is a treasure and will never end.

CHAPTER 2
BECOMING A GROWN UP
SO MUCH TO LEARN

I can remember my first car, the excitement overflowed! I loved that time, I loved that car, it seems so far away. The fun I had behind the wheel I'll share with you today.

Being on the same page, was not always the way, sometimes our parents just don't hear, what you really want to say. I remember a night they just wouldn't give in and made me feel like everything was a sin. I can remember when ...

Friends will come and friends will go, all along the way. We all have stories of things gone wrong, what we could or couldn't say. I remember who was there, almost to the end, something stupid happened and we could never mend. I'd really love to know why this was so, something I guess I'll never ever know.

E ach milestone lived, the changes surround, my body is morphing all over and around. I think the way through this is to try and raise the bar, try to accept ourselves, just the way we are. Some of us struggle, some try to rise above, I'd like to say, no matter what, I try to stay filled with love. Thoughts on self:

Was I adventurous or daring in the things I loved to do? Was I conservative, was I shy or a little bit like you? If I had to describe my personality in a nutshell for all the world to see, here's a few truths I'd be happy to tell a little more about me:

Some of us love High School a little more than the rest, Some of us despised it, barely made it through at best. If I had to describe how it was for me, I'd want to tell the truth for my whole family to see:

Some people are brilliant and quick learning I'd say, there are others more street smart, no books read today! If you asked which category in my life I'd achieved, I'll tell not to judge me, I'm happy and relieved!

Love, love, love, no one teaches us it all, my very first crush was just that I recall. I did have butterflies and the fears that coincide, there were positives and negatives, I would have never passed this by:

Your heart is an organ, you'll need it forever. Be sure to treat yours, like it is your biggest treasure. Sometimes it will hurt, get stomped with words unspoken, my best wish for you, is that yours will never be broken. Mine was.

Did I have any hobbies? What did I love the best? Yes, I had many passions, some were better than the rest. It's good to have hobbies, something we like to do, a way to spend time, a way to feel brand new. I did have a few, and today I will tell, I'd really love to share them with you.

Loss is hard, we all come to see, I was not immune, it certainly happened to me. You can share your life, yourself and your love, but the day will come when we're all called above. The memory of loss that hit me the most was ...

I always hoped for something good, my dreams were always mine. Things don't always work that way, looking back in time. Sometimes life has different plans, other things in mind, sometimes you won't have a choice and leave old hopes behind. A big curve in the road for me was when:

The Bible says we should have nothing to fear, sometimes this changes in every new year. As much as we try to leave worries behind, It's not always easy when our fears come to mind. I always remember being so afraid when it came to:

I was daring, liked adventure, liked new things it's true. But the biggest and bravest feat I've accomplished, I bet you never knew. I was scared, I was nervous but I jumped with both feet, I bet you'd like to know how I didn't skip a beat:

Music is key, a big part of my life, I love how it takes you back. If I could name my top four bands, how do you think they'd stack? I know they made my life complete, I love them still today. Who can they be? What can I say? I'll share my secrets with you today:

Some of us take charge, lead the pack and can be tough. Some are shy or nerdy types who carry so much stuff. I bet you didn't know, the inside of me. Was I a bully? Was I a jock? Keep reading, you will see.

In school we had dreams, we all had our dreams, What did I want to do? Who is the person I wanted to be, I really thought I knew. If I could go back and remember these dreams, I'd know exactly where I wanted to be. Did it happen, am I that person, Let's take a look and see:

As I got older, I became of age, new things were happening in life. My parents didn't always agree with me, they tried to take things in stride. It wasn't so bad until this particular day, there was nothing I could do and nothing I could say.

I talked about a crush, so simple and sweet, but that very first real love, I jumped so high off my feet. So tender and caring, my heart was racing and my knees would bend. My brain felt real foggy, I never wanted it to end.

Thinking back as far as I could, ancestors and relatives, I don't know as much as I should. The most important I remember and as far as I can go, I'd love to share this now, some things you ought to know.

My teachers in high school and in college were great, all teachers were different, they all could debate. We all have the one who stood out from the rest, I'll never forget, the one who was my best! I'll tell you why!

I'm now in love, it's past four dates, I knew on my scale, they measured, they rate. I knew it was love, how did this take place? It was too late to run, I had to embrace. Let me tell you my story:

Books are the bomb, they take me away. Especially as you get older, so many things to say. I do know what I love, what book played a part, of opening my mind and sparking my heart. Let me tell you more:

Fridays would come, we'd all make a plan, we went out to hang, or just see a band. A memory of mine stood out among others, I never made it home that night, never saw my covers.

My early twenties, a roller coaster ride, but always throughout I had someone on my side. They'd guide me along and be sure I stayed on the right road, I'll always be thankful, more than they'll ever know!

My first job was annoying in so many ways, I just had to mention, I just had to say. It was a good job, it taught me a lot, I would love to go back to that job if I could, DEFINITELY NOT! But I loved getting paid at the end of the week, it made me feel valued, in the envelope I'd peek. A spender or saver, do you think you know me, I bet if you guessed, correct you would be:

Some friends went to college, the others did not. The choice I made here, I thought of a lot. The choices I made brought me here to today, If I made them any differently, where would I be, who's to say?

People teach us lessons, all along the way, they come in for a moment and teach us what we know today. If I could go back and thank them for being my greatest fan, I'd thank this person over and over, again, again and again!

Life is stressful no matter your age, finding steadiness and balance, can put you in a craze. Twenties into thirties, I did feel really stressed, looking back in time, I was mostly very blessed.

We all need to unwind, relax and distress, it's hard with our routines to always feel our best. The things I did to do this, may not be right for all, it didn't matter to me one bit, it really was my call.

As we all get older, new things happen every day, I've learn to adjust and bear it all, I have found a way. One thing I love is doing firsts, things I've never done before, the one that stands out the most in life, I loved it to the core.

My thoughts grew more, all on their own. Like a blanket of patches, beginning to be sewn. POLITICS is big, so many disagree, I'll share some of my views, they will help you to see.

Lessons in life, so many to learn, we grab them along the way. The biggest you see, were the ones that showed me how to be a good person every day. I've tried in life to always be true and hoping the person reading this, always does to. Some of the ways I've tried to be a good person in this lifetime.

The number two fear in life is dying, do you know the first? Public speaking in a crowd, said to be the worst. There was a time I had to speak and I almost chose to run, I'll tell you what happened that very day and I'll tell you if it was fun!

My life was flying by, I can imagine for my parents too. What about their parents and then their parents I never knew? I wish I knew more, I wish their past would unfold, these are the things I remember, the things I was told.

By the time I turned thirty, I felt a sense of pride, for all that I've accomplished and surely welcomed the ride. I still today feel very proud when I think of this very thing, I always go back and think of this time and the smiles that it brings.

Being an adult feels so good at times, then more responsibility, then we begin to whine. If I could tell you something never to forget, listen with your head, follow your heart but always trust your gut. And ALWAYS remember:

Broken bones, getting stitches, bumps along the way, it was easier getting hurt in your younger days. Getting older is scary, can be harder bouncing back, be sure to take good care of yourself, stay part of the healthy pack! There was a time I was really hurt/sick, let me tell you more.

By now I had my head on straight, at least I thought I did, I had a slight direction, compared to being a kid. Then suddenly reality hit, I knew nothing all along, as I get older every milestone has a new song. I realized in the grand scheme of things, life is forever a learning experience. I knew this when:

I never did anything illegal (???), although had friends who did, ducking a check, forgetting to pay, was really not this kid. The worst I've done, you will be shocked or maybe you will not. I'll give you the worst that I remember today, the repercussions? Come what may!

After turning thirty, I thought of all the things I've done, as serious as life could be, I still really liked to have fun. Thinking on excitement and where my passions leaned, the things I loved to do in life were exhilarating and obscene! Here are some of the things that really excited me in life:

Some like competition, some kick back and watch. I like to do both, play or hold the stop watch. I'll tell you now what I really like best, jumping in the game or getting extra rest.

Thinking on the town I lived in, it was really pretty cool. My neighborhood was memorable to me, my inner private jewel. What I liked the best was how I'd feel, life in my hometown was unique and very real. Some of the best memories I had were:

I was lucky to get a little travel in, during my younger days, fun with friends and even alone was priceless in many ways. I loved a few trips, more than the rest and will share with you, the ones I loved best:

When I think back, there are a few things I will certainly miss the most. Cartoons and cereal, lots of butter on my toast. Imaginary friends, staying up late and sleepovers with friends will be with me to the end. There is more ...

CHAPTER 3
ALL GROWN UP NOW

Moving out for good was really tough, my very own first place. It didn't matter what I had, even paper plates. I had a job, my couch, my friends, I really never wanted this to end. Some of my best memories were ...

My job, oh my job! Should I stay or should I go? Making right decisions, are they right, we'll never know. That job was good, it payed the bills, it helped me as it should. If I could have changed any part of this, do you really think I would?

My education took its course, sometimes I thought of change. If I could have chosen a different path, I could have re-arranged. I would have studied, I would have learned, I surely could have continued to turn. Do you have any idea what road I would have taken, here's my story straight up and not shaken!

The person I've become, if you only knew. Am I funny or moody, serious or blue? Conservative or bossy, too sensitive at times. Let me tell you this, I'm proud I'm one of a kind.

As I aged and grew more mature, dating began to mean a little more. I became more thoughtful in all the things I planned, their wishes and desires, were soon in my command. My dates were better, much deeper and so true, I'll tell you here, some things I liked to do.

Did I exercise and go to the gym? Was I healthy, lean and trim? Working out is hard, we all know its true, considering my history I'm happy to share, I have a few tips for you:

We all need food to keep us alive, we all need food, just to survive. My favorite food was _____, my favorite drink was _____, and the meal I'd choose most of the time was _____. Are menu's a test? Maybe they are, try to be healthy, just do your very best.

My thoughts on DRINKS:

_____
_____
_____
_____
_____
_____
_____
_____
_____
_____

My thoughts on FOOD:

_____
_____
_____
_____
_____
_____
_____
_____
_____
_____

Friends change in our lives, throughout the years. We cherish them mostly, some bring us to tears. The older we get, the more meaning they bring. They become closer and dear, I'll tell you about mine, both far and near.

When you think of their smile, warm and cozy. Being in nature, cheeks always rosy. When I think of this person, a pleasure to be around, when I hear their voice, what a great sound. I'm so lucky to know them, I'll tell you their name, if they weren't in my life, it wouldn't have been the same.

Sometimes I wish the stars would align and then this person always comes to mind. So good and so kind, always doing for others, I wish I could have helped them more, so sad to watch them struggle. This reminds me of ...

As we age, we get set in our ways but people are weird it's true. Their emotional, crazy and very high strung, I often have to hold my tongue. I try to have patience, I try to be kind, sometimes it doesn't matter, we have our own minds. This thinking takes me back, we need to be aware, I'll tell you a little more, I'll take this time to share.

Many things happen in the course of our life, some are good, some are bad, some are happy, some are sad. When I think of a person older than me, the one I could count on, the one to make me see. I always think of _____, and how much they meant to me.

If I could help the world in some way, I'd probably quit my job and volunteer every day. I'd volunteer in certain groups- Habitat for humanity or serving soup! Do you have a favorite, a one place you'll shine! I'll share with you a few of mine!

I want to describe my first home, did I rent or did I own. No matter where you live, your house should be a home, a place where you can go so you never have to roam. Was my place in the city, the country or no? Maybe in the mountains in a valley who knows. An apartment in a village with walls shades of blue, let me tell you more, I'd love it if you knew!

When I finally met the one, I became two, call it a soul mate, somehow we just knew. Their quality, eyes, demeanor and smile, I knew it was love, I knew it all the while. Here's the story!

I didn't mean to fall in love, it happened very fast. It seemed the dating I did through the years was now a part of my past. I loved the way they looked at me and the way they made me smile, I loved every single piece of them, every single mile! More about _____.

Whether a first love will last or you have many in between, I wouldn't be where I am today, without a love story scene. Was this love the last, did I go on to more? I'll tell you today, a story from my core.

The things we did together, far outweighed my past. I wanted this forever, I hoped that it would last. Of all the things we did together, I remember them so clear. A few of them stand out to me, I'll forever hold them near.

We finally married, the proposal could make you tear, I remember so well, back in the year _____. In case you missed out, in case you weren't there, Nothing would make me happier then to tell the facts and share!

L ife was challenging through the years, we did have laughs, there were many tears. The best of times, too many to post, there's one I treasure and do love the most:

So many stories, a few were bad, sometimes they did, make me real mad. I remember one that took the cake, it lasted many weeks. I don't know how we made it, through that very explosive peak.

In life we learn and create, our own special rituals. Some old, some new, we celebrate through. There were many things we did, to bring in a new life, to share in a Birthday or mourn through a night. Some started as a child, others are still with me today, let me tell you how, we made these memories stay.

Did our marriage last, or end too soon with a twist? Are we still together, or are they ever missed? As I write this today, I'll tell you how I've grown, a very huge part of my life, that I'm happy to have known.

As time went on, we had our share of friends. There were many laughs and fun. Who we were with and what did we do, how did we play and what we all knew? I'd never give up the groups of friends, great memories until the end. Life does change and people go different ways, but the great fun we had, I'd never change those days.

We had a baby and all the good stuff, I loved it all, it was more than enough. Meet my kid(s), you may know them well, their names, all about them, just ask and I'll tell.

Life has changed, I'm sure you know how, diapers and bottles and toys holy cow! They each were so different like carrots and peas, they do have my heart, they bring me to their knees! More about my babies as they grew!

When my children were young it was so loud and so big, school sports and playing, I loved having kids! They grew up so quick, right before my eyes. I never wanted them to leave or ever say goodbye. A favorite story I remember:

I loved helping others and would if I could. My kids, nieces and nephews, their friends, I always would. There was someone special who had a place in my heart, they needed my guidance, right from the start. I hope that I helped in some small way, I love them now, still today.

I love surprises, I think we all do, There was a special time, you may remember too. The occasion was such, all my family and friends, I had the time of my life, all the way to the end.

Vacations are tops, I'm glad I had a few, I was Blessed in my life, my family was too. Of all the places I went, there was a very best, I'll never forget this trip, so much better then the rest!

Food is such a big part of life, a big part of mine, it's true. For years my favorite was number one, a definite go to. What are the things I mostly ate, take out or home cooked meals? These are the things I ate the most, the food that tasted so real!

I wasn't always smart, I don't always know what to do. I certainly made mistakes, and this was a doozy too! If I had a chance to do it over, I would have done just that. I would have been more mindful with my choices, if I can only bring time back.

Was I a good parent, a question to ponder, I think about it often, and wonder. I think I did well, I did the best I could, but if I could do it differently, I wonder if I would.

Death, divorce and struggles, so many in our life. Things happened to our family, some things were not so nice. Most were really, out of our control, a rollercoaster at times. I can't deny it wasn't hard on us, took a toll and weighed heavy on our minds.

L iving in my city, _____, there is so much to do. If you lived here in my time, you would have done them too. If I had more time and could go back if only for a few, the best day trips you could take in my town, let me tell you one or two.

Money was challenging, at times in my life, I managed to make it through. My thoughts on prosperity and abundance you see, I give to you and are definitely free!

If I could have lived life differently, I'm not sure how I would. I think I really liked my life, I'm not sure if I could. Would I have changed any part of this, what would I have found? Would I really want to be someone new and change it all around?

Religious or spiritual, I've looked for the way. I'd like to share, please hear what I say. We're free to believe, any way we choose. I'd like you to know more, I'd love to share the news. I'll tell you now, exactly how I feel, you'd certainly be surprised, I can be very real.

People in my life, have done me right, there have been a few who've done me wrong. Both of these are part of our life, but doing me wrong, is not at all right. There is a person that comes to mind, I really forgive and I choose to move on. I remember when:

The world has changed in so many ways, a lot of it good, some so bad, I hate to say. There have been shootings and destruction, terrorists and more, I've seen some pretty huge happenings, that have shaken me to the core.

We don't always get all the things that we want, but if we could, oh what a joy! If I could close my eyes and have anything I want, I'd give you a list of all my top toys:

In life there are times, we'd love to escape, the daily grind of our days. If I can go to a sacred place, I'm sure you would be amazed. I'd pack a bag and leave today, only if I could, I'd go to the absolute best place on earth, I really, really would.

We all have ideas on the way we appear, some of us an apple, some of us a pear. I've tried to look good, always my best, some would say, don't worry, just get plenty of rest. Looks should not be important and so I'm told, I stand by my opinion, now that I'm old!

Addictions are crazy, sometimes they're by choice. Drugs, Alcohol, foods, all of these can hurt. No one is perfect, we've all had a few faults, a few of mine, I'll break open the vault!

I've been lucky in life and under the stars, to have many nice things, including several cars. I'll tell you about the cars that owned me, will they be around in the future, I guess we'll wait and see.

Events in our life, have changed all the world, 9-11 has happened, Donald Trump and so much more. In case you are reading this in the future that may be, I'm happy to share and give you some history!

In your life, sometimes will be tough, at times you'll feel like you've really had enough. It's so hard to cope, adjust and get by, mostly we want to curl up and cry. If I can leave some advice, when you feel you can't cope, learn from me when you're at the end of your rope.

Some things are crazy, as we all know, people are weird, just go with the flow. Try to be easy and try to adhere, life is too short, we soon won't be here. When you lose patience and just want to cuss, take my advice and don't make a fuss.

If I could write a letter to my younger self, I'd say just keep it together. Don't worry so much, live your days with peace. Live in the moment. Love your life and don't stress any day if possible. You are where your supposed to be and it will all work out in the end. Be your best, do you best and know that ...

CHAPTER 4
THINGS I KNOW FOR SURE

A few things you may not know about me:

My favorite color is:

_____

My favorite animal is a:

_____

My favorite car is a:

_____

My favorite spice is:

_____

My favorite color jellybean is:

_____

My favorite color sheets:

_____

My favorite song is:

_____

My favorite band is:

_____

My favorite ice cream is:

_____

My favorite protein is:

_____

My favorite Carbohydrate is:

_____

My favorite fruit is:

_____

. . .

My favorite sport is:
_____

My favorite TV show is:
_____

My favorite cookies are:
_____

My favorite cuisine is:
_____

My favorite friend is:
_____

My favorite all time comedy is:
_____

My favorite wine is:
_____

My favorite beer is:
_____

My favorite day of the week is:
_____

My favorite restaurant is:
_____

My favorite soup is:
_____

My favorite state is:
_____

My favorite magazine is:
_____

My favorite newspaper is:
___

My favorite beach is:
___

My favorite vacation spot is:
___

My favorite flower is:
___

My favorite plant is:
___

My favorite piece of jewelry ever is:
___

My favorite holiday is:
___

My favorite actor is:
___

My favorite actress is:
___

My favorite job ever was:
___

My favorite board game is:
___

My favorite candy bar is:
___

My favorite candle scent is:
___

My favorite dessert is:

My favorite book is:

My favorite way to exercise is:

My favorite color eyes are:

My favorite topping on pizza is:

My favorite junk food is:

My favorite temperature is:

My favorite toy as a child was:

My favorite TV series is:

My favorite TV game show is:

My favorite soda is:

My favorite color tie is:

My favorite color of clothes to wear is:

My favorite way to have fun is:
___

My favorite sandwich is:
___

My favorite age was:
___

My favorite vegetable is:
___

My favorite religion is:
___

My favorite rock star is:
___

My favorite item in the diner is:
___

My favorite hobby is:
___

My favorite romantic thing to do is:
___

My favorite place to shop is:
___

My favorite lollipop color is:
___

My favorite way to spend a rainy day is:
___

My favorite city is:
___

My favorite sign of affection is:

___

My favorite subject in school was:

___

My favorite neighbor is:

___

My favorite scary movie is:

___

A few additional favorites of mine ...

Movies are a part of the culture in our world, so many, too many, yet we feel we've seen them all. The movies I love, the tops on my list, you have to be sure, the future will never miss!

We all have habits and some of us have quirks, if you don't have any, it's surely a perk. If we all can admit our shortcomings and own up to our messy ways, life could be a little brighter, we can learn a few new ways.

So many people in life, have done nice things for free, some people who have helped me, how nice they were you see. If I could tell them now, I'd show them if I could, I'd thank them kindly and let them know, I'd repay them I really would.

The hardest thing I've ever done, you wouldn't believe it's true. I kid you not, it was really tough, listen up and I will tell you.

We all have a weakness, I know mine for sure. You may not admit yours, but I will tell you more. I am a little weak, in one certain place, you need to know this is true, I definitely tried to find my strength and today I will share with you.

I know there's the law, and we have to follow rules, but if I didn't have to listen, it would be very cool. I'd go into the world, no worries of being caught, I'd let loose, be crazy, and forget what I've been taught. Know what I'd do?

Have you ever had a beef and never cleared the air? If I could tell them now, would they really care? I'd write a note to tell them, I'm not OK at all. I need to vent, I have to yell, I really should cave and make the call! I would write:

Dark rainy days can be just what we need, light a few candles, you'll see what I mean. I'll describe what I'd do on a day like this, how I would spend it and who I'd be with.

I try to do for others, I really want to be good. Because my Mother taught me, because I know I should. One thing I'm really proud of and will shout it from the stars, I'd do it again I promise, this secrets really ours! Something I'm proud of that I've done for someone else:

People make us laugh, people make us smile, a certain person in my life has walked with me the mile. They are funny and crazy, I love how they sound, their the person in my life, I'll always love to be around!

I've been afraid and sometimes scared, we've all been born with fears. I try not to dwell, I try not to care, but they are real and I will share.

Sometimes we know people not connected by blood, It doesn't really matter, we know who we love. As close as any family can be, I'll tell you their names and what they've meant to me.

Making amends, saying sorry, can definitely warm a heart. A phone call or letter, is a wonderful way to start. There may be a person, I need them to see, I am really sorry, please forgive me.

Everything happens for a reason, this I believe is true. Go with your gut and know that the stars are aligned for you. In my life, I can say there are certain things that have happened to me, I'll tell you here, I'd like you to see.

We all feel loved, some times more than others, be grateful every day, for the love that comes your way. Look for love in the little things you do, be appreciative and embrace all the new. Let me tell you from deep in my core, all of things I'm grateful for.

_____
_____
_____
_____
_____
_____
_____
_____
_____
_____
_____
_____
_____
_____
_____
_____
_____
_____
_____
_____
_____
_____
_____
_____
_____
_____

So many important things happen in our lives, it's good to have them in place. I've collected a few for family and friends, for all generations to trace.

Occasion_____Date_____

_____

Occasion_____Date_____

_____

Occasion_____Date_____

_____

Occasion_____Date_____

_____

Occasion_____Date_____

_____

Occasion_____Date_____

_____

Occasion_____Date_____

_____
_____
_____
_____

Let's talk about the way things are, here in 20____.

There are many things in our world today, oh boy you'd be amazed. New products, ideas and businesses, items that are all the new craze. I want you to know about this year, looking back at me, what I'm really putting here, is a thumbprint a stamp, a piece of your history.

A hundred years from now, I really want you to see, what an average day was like for me. I'm sure the world will be different, generations from now, maybe not, you decide, what is so different and how.

I have dreams and hopes for the people I know, my children, my friends, nieces, nephews and more. It's not really my business, I keep it to myself most days, however I'm putting it on paper today.

The Person in My Life:

_____

My Hopes and Dreams For Them:

Where my parents worked may be important to you, here are a few facts about them, you may want to know these too. I may as well throw Aunts and Uncles in here, my brothers and sisters, just so you're aware.

Name: _____

Relationship: _____

Their Profession:

_____

_____

Name: _____

Relationship: _____

Their Profession:

_____

_____

Name: _____

Relationship: _____

Their Profession:

_____

_____

Name: _____

Relationship: _____

Their Profession:

_____

_____

Jokes and pranks can be so much fun, I'd like to tell you all about the one. Was it me who played all the pranks over time, or others who got us almost every single time? I'll tell you a funny story, I'll describe to you the poster, I'll give you all the info, about the family jokester!

Thoughts on education that are very important you see, grammar, high school, trade schools or college, what was right for me? Teachers, subjects, lessons learned, so much for you to know. Let me tell you a little story, my great-great grandchildren, you may want to show.

My thoughts on death and dying, where do we go from here? Do we really turn to ashes or do we float up in the air? Is there really a heaven or is there really a hell? So many thoughts and beliefs, how do we really know?

Did I tell you about my wedding, the day I said "I do"? Did I tell you my soulmate and how I felt so true? The day was so amazing, some things I'd love to tell, from the very morning until late at night and the honeymoon all the way through!

When I think of these words, a few things come to mind, I hope you get to know me just a little more with time.

Fulfilling-_____
_____

Joy-_____
_____

Happy-_____
_____

Exhilarating-_____
_____

Drama-_____
_____

Adventure-_____
_____

Heavenly-_____
_____

Traumatic-_____
_____

Unfortunate-_____
_____

If I had ten thousand dollars to burn, and couldn't pay a single bill, what do you think I'd want to do, how do you think I'd chill? I have a few things on the top of my mind, here are some things you will find:

If I had a few days to go away and do anything I wanted to do, I'd spend it like this, I'd have a great time, if only I could be there with you!

I like to imagine, I like to pretend, I cautiously say it's true, I'd like to share a piece of the fantasy with no one other than you.

If I had to shop for no one but me, my weekly list would probably be the same. I've become accustomed to everyday foods and I doubt they will ever change. My grocery list would look like this:

Memories of sporting events, a day at the spa, a day with the guys, a day with the gals. Some of my most favorite things to do, I'd love to tell you!

If I leave a snapshot for the future years of the kinds of places we go, I'll tell you about stores and restaurants to visit, places you may not know. I wonder if in a hundred years they will have these, or are they rare? Now with this list you'll be able to share and with your family, you can compare.

I may have mentioned this earlier but it may not be very clear, It's very important to leave my health history to carry through the years. Diabetes, heart disease, a little bit high blood pressure, I'll put it here, so the info is very near.

I'm listing medications, all my vitamins to review, I'm also putting here my allergies and other relevant history too. You may not need it, you may not care, but I'm trying to make it easy, so the future is aware. Any special doctors I've had to visit too, just in case, you'll be happy you knew.

A bit of news you may like to know, all over the papers, unbelievable, what a show. There are crazy people all over the world, so near and some really far, the newspapers had a field day, they definitely raised the bar.

Some hints and tips to share on keeping up your home, at my age I know, you can easily look them up on your phone. It's good to know how to care for certain things in life, I may even tell you how, to sharpen your very own knife!

Have I lived my life with purpose all through my journey here? Did I appreciated and live my truth, thrive and really care? Have I reached some goals, achieved my dreams and lived with peace of mind? I know the importance is in not having things, it's about being grateful and kind. A few more things about the real me you need to know...

I**f I had to choose the most defining moment in all of my life, looking back I think it would be

I think of this time because of the deep impact it had through my entire life thereafter. Let me explain:

A few lessons life has taught me on the following:
My chosen profession:
_____
_____

My family life:
_____
_____

My children:
_____
_____

My friends:
_____
_____

My free time:
_____
_____

My adventures:
_____
_____

My love life:
_____
_____

My toys in life:
_____
_____

. . .

If I could have chosen another occupation for my life's work, it would have been:

_____

_____

If I could have chosen a different car, it would have been:

_____

_____

If I could have chosen a different place to visit, it would have been:

_____

_____

If I could have chosen a different place to volunteer, it would have been:

_____

_____

If I could have chosen a different country to live in, it would have been:

_____

_____

If I could have been the CEO of any company in the world, it would have been:

_____

_____

If I could have been a groupie my entire life for a certain band, they would be:

_____

_____

If I could travel the world on a yacht, a private jet, an RV by car or by train, which would it be?

_____

_____

If I could be a Doctor or Lawyer, a Teacher or Politician, a Builder or Real Estate Mogul, a Chef or a Jeweler, a Singer or Artist, which one would I choose?

_____

_____

If I could have cake, pie, chocolate, ice cream or fruit, which would I choose?

_____

_____

If I could have been adventurous and have done one of the following, which one would I choose? A helicopter pilot, a Bakery owner, a Bed and Breakfast owner or a Vineyard owner:

_____

_____

If I had to do one of the following , which would I do and why? A Travel photographer, a zookeeper, a Chocolatier or a Yoga instructor?

_____

_____

When I'm sick, please bring me one of these soups! Chicken noodle, French Onion, Clam Chowder, Tomato or Lentil?

_____

_____

This page? Just venting, here goes!

Astrology! My Birthday is on _____. My sign is _____. I may believe, I may not believe, however horoscopes are in the stars. Our personalities seem to line up with the sign we are given the day we are born. My personality is one, written in the books, listen to this, come take a look.

In my life I've seen some good, I've also seen some bad. I believe there needs to be changes made and this can be very sad. If I were the mayor of my town I'd make a difference and see, how I could make things a little better, I'll show you how it can be.

There are so many illnesses, diseases and more. Why there's so many, no one knows for sure. If I was a brilliant scientist who definitely had a cure, I would spend my days in just one place, curing and healing all. If I could only choose just one, and take that evil away, I'd work with _____, and I'll tell you why today. (Example: Child Cancer, Breast Cancer, Lung Cancer, Pancreatic Cancer, MS, Alzheimer's, Heart Disease, Strokes, Brain Injuries, etc.)

If I had the weekend to spend with my sixteen-year-old niece or nephew, and have real one on one, I could teach them so many wonderful things and how to get life done. I could teach them not to worry and to always try to be kind, I would teach them how to use their brains but always use their mind. I'd guide, support and show them how to drop the hocus pocus, to slow it down, love their life and try to grow and focus. I would also tell them to:

I hope you've had time to read and learn a few different things about me. I hope you pass down a few of my stories for friends and family. Sharing our lives, our stories and our past, is truly how our love can last. Thanks for sharing in my journey. Sending all my love, best wishes and hopes that you will live the best life ever, xo." Just a few final thoughts.

Notes from my Heart

Notes from My Heart

Notes from My Heart

Notes from My Heart

About the Author

New York Based End of Life Doula, Susan Capurso can usually be found researching creative ways in helping people to leave beautiful and memorable legacies for their families, that will be treasured for many generations to come. As an End of Life Doula and Legacy Creator, Workshop Facilitator and Author, her next non-fiction publication brings a plethora of projects and ideas for a person in their end of life journey to implement before they go. Details of Susan's Creative Niche in "end of life", have been published in the New York Post, The Long Islander, Sag Harbor Express and The Long Island Press. Susan's has been featured in several Blogs and Websites including, The National Aging in Place Council and the Pulse Center for Patient Advocacy. As Susan pioneers in our End of Life Growing Movement, she is consistently pursing ways to advocate and support both people in their end of life chapter and your neighbor next door looking to leave their thumbprint in history. Susan's mission is to encourage and guide our world globally in celebrating the lives of over one million people by gifting their life stories and memories into meaningful legacies that will educate and transform the lives of future generations.

Susan is a native of beautiful Long Island in New York and lives with her two sons, Jimmy and Jesse. It was through a series of many losses that led her down a personal journey in her passionate endeavor. So many people leave the world with their knowledge and stories still inside them. Susan feels with a little more mindfulness and pre-planning; our lives will come full circle exactly the way they should. Susan loves travel, beautiful nature, reading and strives to live life in a more peaceful, calm and loving way.

You can contact Susan @

Email – Susan@EastEndDoulaCare.com

Website – www.TheLegacyDoula.com, www.EastEndDoulaCare.com

Phone - 631-946-8100

Facebook @EastEndDoulaCare